Dialectic

Ramya Udaiyar

BookLeaf
Publishing

Presentation by *BookLeaf Publishing*

Web: www.bookleafpub.com

E-mail: info@bookleafpub.com.

ISBN: 9789358731040

First edition 2023

DEDICATION

To my family and dearest friends who inspired me to challenge myself to do something that's totally out of my comfort zone, that is writing poems. This wonderful opportunity by BookLeaf Publishing gave me the space to chew over a few themes that I have been meaning to discuss but never got to say to a wider audience.

Capsized

Greed, corruption, vacillation.
Bursting and slipshod,
Educatees and citizenry,
Left in the dark.
Frenzied steering and,
Dereliction of duty,
All but a recipe for disaster.

One anonymous call,
The beginning of a nightmare.
"Help me.
The ship seems to be sinking."
"What's the name of the ship?"
"Sewol, it's Sewol."
Greed, corruption, vacillation.

Don't move. Stay put. Stand by.
And they run away for their lives.
The dutiful drowned,
The disobedient survived.

"The escape should be made
on the captain's judgement.
Make a decision now."
Interminable correspondence,

Number of passengers,
Currently reported as 450.
Greed, corruption, vacillation.

"What is the captain doing?"
09:47, talked to my daughter on the phone,
09:47, the captain was absconding
concomitantly.
"Follow the teacher's guidance,"
And follow she did.
"I should have told her to escape."
Greed, corruption, vacillation.

Don't move. Stay put. Stand by.
And they run away for their lives.
The dutiful drowned,
The disobedient survived.

More than half, still on board,
Sticking out of the window,
"I heard a chopper and looked out."
Body suspended,
Head supported by the handrail,
It already had a camera, exigently requested.
Greed, corruption, vacillation.

Neither the chopper,
Nor the Patrol Boat 123

called for evacuation.
No sight of rescuers, nor any instructions.
External assistance blocked.
"Mom, dad, the ship has tilted a lot... miss you."
Greed, corruption, vacillation.

Don't move. Stay put. Stand by.
And they run away for their lives.
The dutiful drowned,
The disobedient survived.

"Don't worry, I am wearing a life jacket…
We are all sticking together here."
Fools. They are still waiting for a camera.
The death knell is deafening;
It is tilting again.
Furniture slamming, water gushing in,
Stertorous, Rhonchi, Stridor.

Vehicles cannoning into,
Dash cam quaking and glitching.
Squak and static, indistinct chattering.
The ones supposed to protect,
Absent to lend us a hand.
Only the prow visible now,
Stertorous, Rhonchi, Stridor.

"So, we can presume
there is almost no one

on the ferry then?"
"Yes, yes."

Susurration portentous,
The President playing hooky.
Coast Guards in the fullness of time,
Civilian divers buckled up to dive in.
"There could be some survivors if…"
Pinning hopes on air pockets,
Stertorous, Rhonchi, Stridor.

Snollygosters pump air.
Paraphernalia so dilapidated,
Pretentious and perfunctory,
The President is watching. They staged it.
"You promised to save them,
But you sank the ferry just like that!"
Stertorous, Rhonchi, Stridor.

"So, we can presume
there is almost no one
 on the ferry then?"
"Yes, yes."

Gut-wrenching, diabolical politics,
Civilian divers dive into the unknown.
Breathless, sinister, and murky,
"Many things revealed their struggle to survive."
Shoes a legion submerged, waiting,

For their owners to fill them.
Stertorous, Rhonchi, Stridor.

Dived a million in the next 90 days.
Pupils still locked together in embraces,
'A freeze-frame of panic'.
Long eerie mane drifting in the current.
Recovered hundreds, still possessed by their
ghosts.
"Only if they have saved them..."
Stertorous, Rhonchi, Stridor.

"So, we can presume
there is almost no one
 on the ferry then?"
"Yes, yes."

The Salvage

Yellow, hope for your safe return.
Our aide dead in the water,
Yet, we chased the trauma forevermore.
Howbeit, a decree unforeseen,
Fomented despondency.
A year down we're still investigating.
"May One Small Movement Bring a Great
Miracle."

Kindred, divers, and a republic,
Bawling and mourning, call for action.
Unveiled a truth, so hard to swallow.
Ferry's structure, never could imprison the air.
A smoke screen at its finest,
The government knew it all.
"May One Small Movement Bring a Great
Miracle,"

You say, "I don't remember."
But I remember everything with acute pain.
Then, how come the peers of the realm
claim that you don't know and don't remember?

Yellow, for solidarity and rebellion.
The streets still reek of wick and unburned wax.

Impeach the President!
Won't give up. We're parents.
"I will find out the truth!"
A nation sabotaged by skulduggery.
"May One Small Movement Bring a Great
Miracle."

The court unanimously upholds
To expel President Park.
Uproar, bellowing. whistling,
Exultation, lugubrious, melancholy.
A thousand days from sinking,
Began the salvage of the wreckage.
"May One Small Movement Bring a Great
Miracle."

You say, "I don't remember."
But I remember everything with acute pain.
Then, how come the peers of the realm
claim that you don't know and don't remember?

Flesh and blood of the unaccounted,
Gathered closely, at Mokpo, yet scrambling to
their feet,
At the emergence of the sunken macabre.
Waiting for the mortal remains of their beloved,
Still trapped inside, unable to detach themselves.
Even after death.

"What more do you have to hide?"

Tired of waiting,
Trying to force their way in.
Slamming the gates adorned,
With their ribbons of yellow.
"The kids were killed while waiting.
Don't tell me to wait."
"What more do you have to hide?"

You say, "I don't remember."
But I remember everything with acute pain.
Then, how come the peers of the realm
claim that you don't know and don't remember?

Drilled a scuttle.
Cellular holding selfies,
Now holding a million answers.
Hostage to the trauma,
Kim did away with himself.
A hero, now sung as a patriot.
"What more do you have to hide?"

When we left the scene,
Tiny birds' birdsong,
Oh, so beautiful!
Circling us,
But why does it sound like,
The students wailing and shrieking?

"Asking me not to leave them behind."

You say, "I don't remember."
But I remember everything with acute pain.
Then, how come the peers of the realm
claim that you don't know and don't remember?

Whispers of the Izoku

Quite jarring to my neighbours,
I stick like a sore thumb.
Idyllic and majestic,
Perched on the mystic green,
On the steep slopes of,
The Mountain of the Whale.
Overseeing the ruins,
Of the decimated,
On the coastal town of Otsuchi.
Mollified by Sasaki,
I see the wood for the trees.
My pristine glass walls,
And ebony rotary dial,
Sitting next to,
My dainty little notebook.
Pride myself on,
Carrying voices into the wind,
For I'm among,
The Earth's most formidable
sites of resilience.
What they wouldn't give,
For that one last conversation.
Silently engulfing the knots,
In the stomachs of the bereaved.
Oh, I feel like a parent!

When I see my children,
Dawdle towards me.
Don't concern yourself,
If you can't reach my door,
For your odyssey is proof enough,
Of your intrepidity.
Listen to the psithurism,
Lose your gourd,
Wear the green willow.
Manifest and imagine,
Flutter your wings,
And break this chrysalis.
Shake like a leaf,
To turn over a new leaf.
Sometimes a 'metaphysical grieving space',
While other times a shrine.
My pilgrims visit me,
From far and wide.
From Australia and the Philippines,
To Holland and Spain.
From Korea and China,
To Syria and Namibia.
Some enter in pursuit of answers,
Others in desiderium,
Still others, to chirp that,
They're alive and well.
Because the perished are still,
Very much a part of the family.
As Sasaki puts it,

"No matter how hard it is,
Hope makes life worth living."

Maimed

Gleefully chattering,
Running through the corridors,
Scribbling with chalks,
On charcoal slates,
Without a care in this world.
Friends with dozens,
Now counting on fingers.
Haven't got a clue,
How they disappeared,
Into thin air?
Was only six, when I was,
Playing in the field,
With my little sister,
When our aunt lured us,
In the deceit of someplace nice.
As little kids do,
We tagged along too,
The minute we entered,
What looked like a downtrodden home,
A woman clutched us,
Obscuring our view,
With a scruffy blindfold.
Our squeals falling on deaf ears,
Roped us to a fence.
Judders of drums,

Along with ceremonial songs,
Sung by the coffin-dodgers,
Ringing to my ears.
A brilliant excuse for chicanery,
To camouflage the background noise,
Of blood-curdling screams,
From juvenile girls.
Feeling sick to the stomach,
It was a fait accompli.
Once the blindfold was gone,
The panorama scared,
The Bejesus out of me.
Naïve young girls bleeding,
Howling from pain.
A fearsome old doyenne,
Inched towards me,
Wielding a paring knife,
So sharp and gory,
Already stained with the blood,
Of those weeping colleens.
In a flash of light,
A trio of women,
Immobilized me.
Perplexed, I kicked the air,
A surly woman unexpectedly accosted,
And sat right on my chest,
Covering my mouth.
With her eyes emotionless,
The wielder said,

"It will be over in a jiffy."
Empty. I wasn't a human for them.
Stripped from my underpants,
I yelped as I felt,
A searing pain.
I was cut down there,
And laid torpid.
All left to bleed,
Into dirty little caverns.
Later, they took us,
Back to our slayer,
Crowded into one room to heal.
For a quarter they 'treated' us,
Sans a doctor.
Silenced to never mention,
About our purgatory.
My mother was elated,
An expectant hush to pick us.
"Where were you when they
circumcised me?"
"Shush, keep it quiet."
Days passed and my sister,
Succumbed to her misery.
Apathetic to her ruination,
They threw the village a feast,
And arranged my matrimony to a gaffer.
"She was blamed for not surviving,
And I was praised for taking it well."
I was finally a woman.

Pure and virgin.
Stitched for his intense pleasure.
A lovely flower obliterated,
For no reason at all.
As "Tradition is not easy to slay.
Slaying young girls is."

Weaving Hope

Jeered as distracting,
Cavilled as unkempt and matted.
Reek of patchouli and weed,
Pleased as punch after,
Juxtaposing to sheep's wool,
Vindicating your swelled head.
My thick textured locks,
A definite bruise to your ego.
Repudiate to throw in the towel,
And acquiesce to your,
Eurocentric standards.
Whited sepulchres.
Black cornrows rebuked,
Meanwhile, the audacity to,
Sensationalize Bo Derek's.
A talking point on front covers,
Malevolence sticking out a mile.
Easy fad for culture vultures.
Not their fault, it's penury of the psyche.
Honour, what literally meant,
The difference between life and death.
Cornrows, dreadlocks and twists,
Indicative of one's identity,
Kinship, ethnicity, age and beyond.
Timeless rock arts of Algeria,

The Tassili plateau of the Sahara.
Weaves thriving a community,
A catharsis for femme.
Reminisce the Middle Passage?
Things get swept under the rug,
To protect the image.
Scalps shaved to enslave.
Dehumanizing headwraps,
The most claustrophobic stranglehold.
Extirpated by the captors,
Saw a messiah in Bioho.
Propounded a map of tresses,
A clandestine attempt at liberation.
Sisters' departes now mapping,
Routes of brave escape.
Bantu, now a mountain,
Tropas, now troops.
Ingenious stashes for seeds,
Gold nuggets and weapons.
Believing to build,
A future of sustenance.
'Tejiendo Esperanzas'.
To all the black fellas,
Wear your crown with pride,
Your braids matted from resilience.
If ever a mortal,
Has the temerity to do,
A disservice to the African heritage,
San Basilio de Palenque,

Will come to your rescue.
Relent to toe the line.
"(Y)our coils hold,
The DNA of survivors."

Kintsugi

Sometimes a pear,
Other times a mango,
Still others a strawberry.
Hips fuller and,
Breasts thick as thieves.
Anatomy is curvylicious,
Not your typical
36-24-36.
Hourglass, a dime a dozen.
Love handles, cellulite and,
A flabby stomach is my fashion.
My ears are itching,
From your jibes on fat-shaming.
Scooped an extra serving,
Can already see those cogwheels turning.
Why the sudden concern,
For my longevity?
For my tryst with matrimony?
I have nothing but,
Scorn for you.
My slender sibling,
Always been a barometer,
To mock my extra pounds.
Missy's a big eater,
Still, I'm accused of starving her,

Of stealing from her plate.
Pandered to your every whim.
Vigorously toiled,
To shed them pounds.
Pulled a muscle,
Floated like a feather.
Old tight garms,
Now fitted like a glove.
You gave a stink eye.
Were already breathing down,
A newly-weds neck,
For bearing kids sooner.
Was minding my own business,
But you pulled me into,
That bane of a conversation.
Advised the bride,
To be as plump as I am,
When she will be heavy with child.
You said your piece.
A kick in the teeth.
Was ready to crumble to pieces,
At the first touch.
I had decided then,
To grow a thick skin.
Not waiting for the world,
To change and accept me,
For what I am worth.
My body isn't an invitation,
To get mocked by others.

"The self-righteous scream judgments
against others to hide the noise
of skeletons dancing in their own closets."
My curvy beauties,
Don't sell yourself so short.
The crescendo would for sure,
Will chew your ear off,
But bear in mind,
They know nothing about you,
Nor your might.
Those who mock you,
For your pain and challenges,
Aren't worth a wee bit of your attention.
Go indulge in that,
Heavenly decadence.
If anyone has quibbles,
They have to lump it.
Their worthless two cents,
Shouldn't wither us anymore.
Because our stretch marks,
Are now an art of kintsukuroi.

Komorebi

Be mindful of the times,
When you felt absolutely free.
Liberated, unrestrained, and unbridled.
It could be in the safety of a concert,
Where you felt belonged and understood.
In staying up belatedly,
After the sun has gone down,
And having a meaningful,
Heart-to-heart with your buddies.
In a verdure meadow,
Or a forest clearing,
Lying with your back on the floor,
Overseeing a fulgent night sky.
In the company of resounding abstraction.
In a moment of epiphany.
In doing mundane chores, unrushed.
In a breath of fresh air,
While clearing your mind.
In screaming one's head off,
Standing on the precipice of a summit.
In enjoying a cheap thrill in all honesty.
In enjoying a straightforward comedy,
Guilt-free of dialectical thinking.
In the impermanence of abstinence.
Because it is only fair that,

You comprehend the signs,
To slam that brake.

Tableaux Vivant

He found her numinous and witchy.
She found him fierce and exhilarating.
It was a karmic acquaintance.
Conspicuously congruous physiognomy,
Like the universe had warped,
For the inception of a tantric collaboration.
The beginning of an oeuvre,
Lionised for posterity.
Manifestation of an iconography,
Germinating from a fervent,
Convoluted liaison.
One woman and one man,
Melding the amalgamation,
Into the third element.
A hermaphrodite 'that self,'
Virgin of envenomed ego.
Crude uncoerced abuse,
Pensiveness, endurance, abstinence,
A comfortable tension,
Sustaining the equilibrium of,
The female and male principles.
Uncontaminated from doubt,
Uncontaminated from suspicion.
Their hearts no longer,
Belonging to self but shared.

Motionless nights spent,
In the solitude of the Australian desert,
Sealing any trepidations.
What a shame!
The very antithesis,
Of their fusion,
Infiltrated the cosmos, Ego.
Their doom was thus fixed.
The Great Wall that was,
Avowed to be their Altar,
Trivialized into dissolution.
Intimacy lost to infidelity.
Trust lost to indolence.
The last embrace now,
Drained out of warmth.
The lovers lost to comrades.
Marina lost to Ulay.

Beasts of Burden

Never make their bed.
Got clothes everywhere.
Won't budge to do the dishes.
Not once volunteered to toil.
Always warming the cushions,
Scot-free and carefree.
Cranking up the volume,
Until the television is too loud.
As if to make a mockery,
Of sharp sexism and,
Your tokenistic equality.
Glorification of self-sacrifices.
Demonisation of self-care.
Gaslit to search,
A purpose in wifehood,
Distancing the mirage,
Of a parallel universe.
The famed Indian hospitality,
A smokescreen for,
Invisible labour.
Women attending to,
The behests of their sons,
Partners, parents, and in-laws.
Worked her fingers to the bone,
To feed their guests,

Without a courtesy,
As to give a heads-up.
Conditioned to crave,
Male validation,
While going through cycles,
Of invalidation herself.
A numb urge to give up,
Evermore trying to be understanding,
But never being understood.
Spaces gendered,
To enforce stereotypes.
Domesticated to find,
Ecstasy in housewifery.
Burned out, indisposed and depressed.
But what about the
squalor in my heart?
When all is said and done,
Women are nothing but,
Just beasts of burden.

Where on God's Green Earth…?

It's the screeching noise,
From the wheels of my heart,
Grinding to a halt.
Mind going a mile a minute.
Each time I remain enchanted,
By your off-kilter beauty.
The obvious is too ostentatious.
It's as if time stills for us,
Encasing in a bubble,
With just the two of us.
The rest is just background noise.
The hyphenation between us,
Contracting. My visceral fear,
Trying to nudge me,
Out of my reverie.
Mocking my hankering,
For wish fulfilment.
But as if I was,
A reading in the tea leaves,
You shoot an irresistibly,
Reassuring smile.
Revivifying me akin to a defibrillator.
Your sanguine gait, so suave,
Drawing me like,

A compass to its true north.
Only a hair's breadth away.
Begrudgingly resisting,
To foist me on you.
Am I being perspicacious,
For seeing your diffidence?
I can see a maelstrom whirling,
In that pretty skull of yours.
Like clockwork, one hand resting,
On your heart, while the other,
Locking your fingers.
Can see your pupils dilate,
An uncharacteristic caesura,
Breaking the rhythm of your heartbeat.
Whatever infinitesimal distance,
Now vanishing into a passionate kiss,
Rapturously beaming to the hiccup,
Only I am privy to.
You had faltered.
You feel like a ridiculous pipe dream.
As if grasping my apprehension,
You delve in more deeply,
If that's even possible,
Fogging me with breathlessness.
Knackered and deceived,
By your subterfuge,
And mellifluous giggles.
Swinging our inextricable arms,
You lead me to uncharted zones,

Oblivious of your triumph,
In dousing my soul on the conflagration.

Unrequited Sapphic Love Story pt.1

Generous to a fault.
The virtue of being kind,
In an unkind world.
Can't help my strong aura.
Sweet as honey and,
Hot as the Sun.
Attractive to swarms,
Like a moth to a flame.
Evidence of my promiscuity,
In the trail of hickeys,
Now painting my body.
Hypnotising you with essential oils.
Your noise, high-pitched and whiny.
Beet red and puffy.
Sending shockwaves through all of you.
I'm having a whale of a time.
It's a numbers game after all.
Smells like acrid and a slaughterhouse.
Laughing like a maniac.
Is this emancipation from adultery?
There was no romance in the air,
Just a bevy of pesky mosquitoes.
Bloody suckers, the bane of my life.
Kin exploit as a bait,

To shield themselves from,
A mozzie misery.
Bloodstain on my shirt,
Molehills on my skin.
Always swatting, stamping, and flailing.
My predicament pales,
In comparison to these voracious moochers.
Covered from head to toe,
I feel like a prude.
Still managed to fly up,
The legs of my jammies.
You libidinous pest,
Trying to reproduce a village.
Giving in to my twisted fate,
I try to get some shut-eye,
While you suck and munch on me,
In my sleep, making a mental note,
To add that hazmat suit to my cart.

Unrequited Sapphic Love
Story pt.2

No peace, even in the
privacy of my bath.
Lusting on my birthday suit,
Always ready to jump my bones.
God bless the vanguard,
Of my knight in shining armour.
Scampering to find it,
Water dripping from,
My voluptuous body,
Leaving a mess.
There it is! The mosquito racket.
The sight of it had,
Never been this arousing.
Swinging it on autopilot.
How I haven't yet electrocuted myself,
Is still astounding to me.
Frolicking when I try,
To gobble a morsel.
I would swallow some of you,
For sure, someday.
I am not even an 'O'.
Can't ever dare to dream,
About wearing those comfy hot pants.
Alas, the writing is on the wall.

I raise my hands in annoyance.
Much to my chagrin, these vampires,
Are now a part and parcel of my life.
Lest the government declares them vermin.
Until then, I'm better off with my zapper.

Listening to My Inner Child

My inner child remembers,
My thatha-paati igniting,
A heap of coconut shell shards,
And dried old leaf stems for ablution.
It remembers those monthly halves,
During school and the cheeriness,
Anticipating the bonus play hours.
It remembers my smiling Amma's
star-shaped dosas,
While my sibling and I,
Row over giving her directions,
From our island seat.
It remembers my neighbours,
Jostling to take turns,
To play Duck Hunt,
On our old box computer.
It remembers my Amma,
Calling our childhood friend,
After a fun-filled yoga session,
To slurp on some piping-hot Maggi,
On-time to watch,
Our favourite show as a kid- M.A.D.
It remembers my Akka climbing,
On my Appa's shoulders,
As he lifts his plate,

To let her chug Amma's rassam.
It remembers Amma riding her moped,
To pick us up from school,
Meanwhile, other kids gaped at her in
admiration.
It remembers my Appa swinging us,
On his chubby yet strong biceps.
It remembers me tailing my Akka,
While playing hide and seek.
I used to be her shadow back then.
It remembers me celebrating,
My birthday on Akka's day,
As mine falls during the holidays.
We tricked our schoolmates,
Into thinking we were twins,
As we occasionally twinned our outfits.
It remembers a million other memories,
Conjured up by my olfactory sensation,
By our old photo books,
By places that hold nostalgia.
My inner child brims with joy,
When I evocate the past.
It feels belonged,
When I get through to someone.
I can hear its frail timbre,
Seeking to grab my attention.
It's nodding in affirmation.
I just need to listen,
To the little one, inside me.

A Dime for Every Musing

Have you ever stopped in your tracks,
And marvelled at a passing beauty?
Ogled at their incandescent nimbus?
Redolent of those Rubenesque women.
Unapologetically assertive.
Strutting, without a care in this world.
Recklessly heedless about,
The imprisoning gaze of society,
Eyeing her like a piece of meat,
Or an object of ridicule.
All for choosing to wear scanty,
And carrying it effortlessly.
Blurring them like a focal zoom,
Exuding that main character's energy,
I look at her awestruck.
In my state of Niksen,
I lose track of her silhouette.
Rewinding the memory,
I try to hold my shoulders back.
Ruminating over,
The weight of my intrusive thoughts,
Will I ever be that confident in my skin?
Will I ever be able to celebrate,
The whole of me?

Damned if You and Damned if You Not

Barely managing to set foot,
On the cramped local,
Dodging through the crowd.
Avoiding any dangling,
Sweaty armpits, like a plague.
Knew for a fact that,
Finding a vacant fourth seat,
In the wee hours of the day,
Is wishful thinking but,
Holding on to that last sliver of hope,
I bask in the soothing notes of,
KK, Bombay Jayshree, and ARR,
Whilst looking out, hawk-eyed,
For that highly covetable yet,
Claustrophobic fourth seat.
Commuters scooting and,
Switching at every station,
While I have aged 10 years,
Waiting for my turn.
Halfway through, I am finally seated.
Mentally cursing at my long femurs,
For getting in the way of,
Testy obnoxious aunties.
Amid all the histrionics,

The hijras sashay through the commotion.
The mob clearing the way.
To escape their clutches.
Draped in shimmery sarees,
Faces coated with cakey makeup,
Clapping tin tali and singing songs.
Bestowing unsolicited and,
Sometimes gratuitous blessings,
In exchange for money.
I can see them in my periphery,
Gradually approaching my row.
My body goes rigid.
I was anything but scared.
It is the vacillation about,
Not denting their dignity.
Will my alms aid for their upkeep?
Or will they sustain their misery?
Will they assist,
In their fights for equality?
Or will they enforce,
The entrenched societal norms?
I will be damned if I and damned if I not.
By then they are off the local.
Leaving me to come to grips with,
my catastrophic train of thought,
While everyone else goes about their lives.

Drop that Fig Leaf

My darling, drop that fig leaf.
That's a double entendre.
Your bashfulness is in full glory,
Still, you accepted the invitation with alacrity.
You are Almighty's magnum opus.
Possessed of such Duende,
That no sane organism,
Is unable to look away.
My modest violet,
You may seem laconic to some,
But I can see it,
In your loving gaze,
In your dulcet voice,
In your melodious giggles,
In your silent acquiescence.
Leading me in a rhapsody,
Lingering for the remainder of the day.
Running my fingers through,
Your bouncy, velvety waves,
Subconsciously practising Cafuné,
While you chant about your day,
With meticulous detail.
Your cologne wafting over to my side,
Intoxicating. I'm high on dopamine.
Only catching the end of your sermon.

Realising, you throw a jab at me,
And get a few jabs back.
Your existence's got,
A strong purchase on me.
You guffaw at my stupidest jokes,
That anyone with a modicum of
common sense will roll their eyes.
You are a far cry from,
My blast from the past.
Found me in a more equal relationship.
Your aftertaste's a chalice of ambrosia,
Conferring immortality to my soul.
Small things I didn't give,
A second thought about,
You took so much pleasure in.
Sometimes, I wonder, if you are just,
A figment of my imagination.
But the warmth emanating,
From your bone-crushing embrace,
Interrupts my wool-gathering.
Oh darling, let me fall into the abyss,
Of your obsidian doe eyes.
So please, drop that fig leaf.

Nationalism

BONUS pt.1
(My first attempt at poetry, when I was less than
15 years old.)

Uncontrollable cases,
A wild goose chase.
No use for the people,
Only importance to personage.
What's the use of this freedom,
When only nationalism?

God holds us in their right hand,
But civil wrecks imbalance.
What's the use of this freedom,
When only nationalism?

March due to corruption,
Strikes due to inflation.
Strains of blood lost to terrorism.
Inequality, far and near.
Will the nation progress?
Will the stomachs of the poor fill?

There's a question on every lip,

When no one remembered,
Courageous freedom fighters.
Not even the soul is left.

The high is ruptured,
The low is left poor.
No idea except for Indians,
To fight another war.
What's the use of this freedom,
When only nationalism?

Writing a Letter in the Language of Flowers

BONUS pt.2
(Written when I was 16.)

To my light purple Lilac,
How are you?
I'm writing this letter as blue Salvia.
I'm pink Camellia.
I desire some Balloon Flowers,
As I Primrose.
Daffodil and yellow Tulips.
I want you to Mistletoe.
Sweet Pea, I'm yellow Lily.
Pink Carnation.
Let's wish for Baby's Breath and Chamomile.
White Clover and Azalea.
Basil, red Chrysanthemum.

Yours faithfully,
Your Purple Rose.

(Translation)
To my first love,
How are you?

I'm writing this letter as I think of you.
I'm longing for you.
I desire for you to re-enter my life,
As I can't live without you.
The sun is always shining when I'm with you.
There's sunshine in your smile.
I want you to kiss me.
Thank you for the lovely time, I'm walking on
air.
I'll never forget you.
Let's wish for everlasting love and patience in
adversity.
Think of me and take care of yourself.
Good wishes, I love you.

Yours faithfully,
Your love at first sight.